ALSO BY ANNE CARSON

Red Doc>

Red Doc>

ANNE CARSON

VINTAGE CONTEMPORARIES

Vintage Books

A Division of Random House LLC

New York

FIRST VINTAGE CONTEMPORARIES EDITION, MARCH 2014

A portion of this work first appeared in *Harper's* (February 2013).

The Library of Congress has cataloged the Knopf edition as follows:
Carson, Anne.
    Red doc> / Anne Carson. —1st ed.
      p. cm.
    1. Stesichorus. Geryoneis—Adaptations.   2. Epic poetry, Greek—Adapations.
    3. Monsters—Poetry.   I. Title.
      PS3553.A7667R43 2013   811'.54—dc23   2012032322

Vintage Trade Paperback ISBN: 978-0-307-95067-3
eBook ISBN: 978-0-307-96059-7

Book design by Cassandra J. Pappas

www.vintagebooks.com

Printed in the United States of America

for the randomizer

Try again. Fail again. Fail better.

—SAMUEL BECKETT, *Worstward Ho*

Red Doc>

Red Doc>

GOODLOOKING BOY wasn't he / yes/ blond /
                                yes / I do vaguely
                                / you never liked
                                him / bit of a
                                rebel / so you
                                said / he's the
                                one wore lizard
                                pants and

pearls to graduation / which at the time you admired /
                                they were good pearls /
                                you said he reminded you
                                of

your friend Mildred / Mildred taught me everything I
                                know she taught me how
                                to entertain / you must
                                miss

her / I miss her martinis [stubs cigarette] so what's he
                                up to now / just got out of
                                the army / wounded /

    messed up / are they giving him care / a guy shows
                                up with a padded envelope
                                of drugs every night I
                                guess

it's care / he staying with you / for a while / behaving
                                himself / some days he sits
                                around reading Christina

    Rossetti some days he comes out of the bathroom
                                covered in camouflage
                                paint / keep him away
                                from

your herd / did I tell you I finished Proust / oh yes /
seven years / can you
reach me

those matches behind you / reading it every day /
thanks / was like having
an extra unconscious /
well I'm

not fond of those multivolume things / there's the
part where he's comparing
his Tante Léonie to a
waterlily /

she's a swimmer / no she's a neurasthenic / I don't get
it / well she's old nervous
lives in a single room
trapped in her little

train of habits the pills the pains the spying out the
window / hmmm / a
waterlily caught in a
current he

says / could be too late for me to appreciate Proust on
the other hand I'm at a loss
I've read all the Len

Deightons in the library / hundreds of people visit his
home every year some just
burst into tears / Len

Deighton / no Proust / say remember that time we
were driving and crashed /
what time / I forget where
it was I

was driving no you were driving I was looking out
the window all of a
sudden I thought I saw a
deer racing

out a driveway so I start to just then my brain flashes
on it being a wooden lawn
ornament not a real one

WATCH OUT FOR THAT WOODEN DEER I
yelled so loud you drove
off the road into a guy's
hedge and

burst into tears [she laughs he laughs] / speaking of
tears / listen [gets out a
cigarette] to that wind /
storm coming / or is it the
traffic / wind I think /
from the north sounds like
/ so your surgery is
scheduled

for when / the 25th / you want me to come with you /
no dear / well if you
change your mind / I
won't

change my mind / I can easily / thanks though / well
/ [glances down at her
crossword] I'll be fine /
well so / time for you to
go / I'll call on the
weekend / take some of
those apples they're the
kind you like

WIFE OF BRAIN

we enter we tell you
we are the Wife of Brain
at this point you have little grounds to complain we say
a red man unfolding his wings is how it begins then the lights
come on or go off or the stage
spins it's like a play *omnes*
to their places
but
remember
the following faces
the red one (G)
you already know (what's he done to his hair) his old friend
Sad
But Great
looks kind
beware
third Ida Ida is limitless and will soon be our king
scene is
a little red hut where G lives alone
time
evening

everyone always angry on TV. He shuts it off and pulls the plug. On his way to the underpass with the TV a deer leaps out. All stop as if condensed. A wild cracky sound is up first in birds overhead then comes down and the deer has it four times like a rock sneezing. G moves the deer ripples off into fog and night. He stands listening. Volume and echo drip in the underpass. He is balancing the TV on a bit of ledge. Gravel shifts behind him. Perhaps the deer.

NOT THE DEER she hits him a whack with a 2 × 4 down he goes his poor poppystalk bent oddly sideways. Thought you were after my hiding place she says. How he met Ida. The sound of the deer still raw in his lobes when he wakes the next day. She has brought him to a bright fire and a white fresh floor. Underpass traffic roaring somewhere. Her near the wall. Her hand on his brow. Another free dawn she says laying a rag on the headache oh. Vinegar smell. Right angle he thinks. Thanks. Say thanks. Lashing spokes spin in his brain so he lies still and dreams of the leafless tree and the absolute unobstructedness of light that fell through it a dream he'd had before. An April dream.

EVER SHE SAID to G and his brother after their father died. I don't want to live with either of you ever. I'll move some place hard for you to get to. And she had. Taps her ash. They are at the kitchen table. Not the same kitchen but the same old yellow Formica table he used to do his homework at. Fifth grade learning the kings of England she sat by him each gray morning with her ashtray her red velour bathrobe going over the list. Kings and mornings blend in his mind with scenes from *I Love Lucy* maybe it's the bathrobe maybe the kitchen table in its alcove. She is talking about the garden club. Pruning the lilacs her. Physical therapy people who've died he tells her his old friend is back and has a new name. They discuss names. She has the newspaper open and reads out letters from the Help column *I am an intellectual giant* begins one. They laugh.

Laughing with your mother. Coming out of the lake into a big towel and her arms. They haven't always talked easily. He used to think it would improve with age but lately she seems ever more bored by him. Than usual. He watches her face. Avoids detail. To simply say what comes to mind to simply float. Sometimes this does happen.

he doesn't let the herd eat the forsythia but knows they like to be amidst its blazing yellows. He stands they graze he watches. Ida watches. She puzzles him he puzzles himself. Her old plaid sportscoat his tendency to befriend catastrophe. She is innocent and filled with mood like a very tough experimental baby. Her drawing book open on her knees. Blackish iridescent hides shine green as sharks amid the herd. A lone white one (Io) glows like an idol and is Ida's favorite. She looks at her drawing looks back at Io sets her drawing book down on the grass. They smell she says. Why they're called musk oxen he says it's in a gland by the knee. What is? The musk. Some people hate it he says. You ever see a musk ox dip its head to touch its knee get out of the way it's going to charge but Ida is no longer listening. The oxen move slowly. They chew coarse gaps in the weeds shifting ever so slightly sideways with their great brows bent and the long fur sweeping their ankles. Each head has two horns that part as neatly as a boy about to play the piano wets his hair and hopes it stays flat for the whole recital. G faintly smiles. It's their looking down he loves the steady way they pay attention downward yet are watching everything else too. A musk ox can see 310 degrees around in a circle. Like cats he thinks. Like cats Ida says. What? Look easy to draw but it's so not true. Ah he says. I don't hate it she says but G is frowning now. His wings are rising up on his back and he wants to know why.

BIG GOLD LION head comes loping along. Army pants bare chest barreling down the towpath just misses Ida. She yells and jumps. Takes on a glow. There she goes scrambling onto Io. Wait a minute says G. Ida is kicking Io's sides urging the great white bulk to move. It doesn't move. It hoists its huge head around and gives a What now? look at Ida's exalted foot dangling there it's hard to believe this gnat is pesking her. Then some inside switch flicks on. She is a beast constructed for smooth striding. Now long pelvic muscles organize her and the vast loosejointed shoulders glide forward into movement. *I'm a ride a white ox uptown and see how I mix!* Ida calls back and has the wit to tuck her knees under the ears. G stands watching people dodge sideways off the towpath. Something more than Ida has moved out of his control.

shock the boy the man he knows him. Knew. The lion head the sloping run a lavishness in him made you want to throw your soul through every door. Memory sucks it all backward. Hands and no place for hands last morning later you realize that was our last. Take my. Fuck. Tiled floor a suitcase standing bleeding no thank you yes. No. Yes. Thin red tracking no. Yes. Your nose is he says. Take my white skin yes take it my astonishing morning it's fine. Bleeding he says. The other. Last. No. Yes. No. Take it. My handkerchief. Fine. What if he does. Your taxi is here. Who says this. Your redletter brain as you struggle and sift longlost puns comes a torrent of noise each cell shimmying on its little mitochondrial hilt. Pure energy there. Memory is exhausting. G sits down on the ground. The man had been his oxygen once. When he left there was no oxygen.

But cell death can confer advantages. Differentiation of the fingers and toes occurs in a developing human embryo because cells perish in these places. We all make good use of separate digits in our life but then (so Proust) catch sight of an old glove and burst into tears. G weeps thinking of Proust. The oxen arrive softly around him.

Wife of Brain

hits the floor if a Truck
backfires can't
stand
the smell of diesel or rain in May you ever see
their orders were to mow the children no one
let A pig in the shape of a down pig Bleed would he
Ever *let* a pig bleed to
spared at such evening your nightfall bleed drugs in
they
come with the death in a padded bleed
he said sweet
mead *I have to*
Let the pain the blades the steeds the brittle children
carving
Vicodin methadone Paxil *let* a big X
Drank
out a nightfall across his belly
let Cut
sweet Out
the pain out

in the waiting room he enters she is sitting. He doesn't remember it she always will. He doesn't see the nurse coming down the hall she does. He doesn't notice the other one the stacked trays the syringes rounding the corner just as the nurse and they collide. Trays syringes fly crash she thinks oh no. He hits the floor in a crouch her heart is going fast. His ragged eyes pouring in every direction fists up neck shiny with sweat her watching fear judder to a halt all over his body. Both blush. He laughs and gets up she looks away. He has pissed himself she bends over her drawing. *Suppose a lone man.*

YOU   A   TUESDAY

appointment like me / I
guess / always writing in
that book / not writing
drawing / drawing what /
my sunny

self / got a name / Ida / I'm
Sad / why / no it's my
name Sad But Great
capital *S* capital *B* capital
G people call

me Sad / that some type of
indigenous name / army /
army make you have a
certain name / make you
have a

certain everything / how /
orders / but your name is
your fate can't take orders
on that / no / no / so what's

Ida mean fatewise / Ida
means *idea* / who told you
that / Greek guy he says
Ida is a verbal word for the
way

you see inside your mind /
no shit / that's the gist / so
look at me Ida what do
you see inside your mind /
see a hole right through
the middle of you

THEY DO NOT
talk more that day.

SO THEY'RE RED / no / is he
red / yes / wings / yes /
okay I do know this guy /
from the army / [laughs] /
what's funny / idea of him

in the army / why'd you
enlist / oh people thought
I'd be better off / off / I was
getting into mischief /
people

like who / Dad / mischief
like what / is this an
interview / I like to close all
the loops / here's the thing
Ida either we

sit here and close loops or
we go stir up some shit /
shit like what / where'd
you say he keeps this herd
/ down by the overpass /
well that's it then

HAVE THE DUSK
deepen. Equal trouble.
The one helpful thing she
said to him that summer
whether you keep this man
in your life or put him out
equal trouble. Is it the
adverbs. Have the mother
speak have the boy speak.
In. Out. Years ago. All
those darlings. Out where.

WIFE OF BRAIN

not Ida's idea but nonetheless to
introduce her two new friends the one
a lonely herdsman the other kind of
messed
up by war but having
realized at once when
she got
to the little red door &
heard the word *You!* said by both gentlemen with
simultaneous
stress her own
redundancy she called out *Shoot*
I'm as hot as a rat in a wool sock and
vanished *ad hoc*

TYPICAL NIGHT-HERDING SONGS gallop their rhythms and tell of love. G doesn't usually sing to the herd at night. He may talk to them listen stand in the herd. Listen. That community. A low purple listening but with a height to the sound. Them listening. They direct it up and out. They stand in a circle facing away from the center (calves in the center) and the long guard hairs hang down to brush their ankles like pines. Like queens. Like queens dressed in pines. Musk oxen are not in fact oxen not castrated bulls nor do their glands produce musk. Much is misnomer in our present way of grasping the world. But pines do always seem queenly as they sway so grand and anciently from the sky to the ground. Motion is part of listening. As the night goes on let's say he's there for a number of hours the motion changes. At first they just shudder a bit like any large entity come to rest but gradually imperially they begin swaying. Then as one rhythm they pass the sway from shape to shape around the circle its amplitude increasing its warmth rising from knees to hearts to eyes its pressures rolling across the large loose joints of the shoulders and down the long bones of the hips until at some point with a phrasing as simple as a perfect aphorism one of them spins up off its shanks and performs a 360-degree spin in air and returns to place. Slotting itself into the undulation of the others as firmly as *temptation* into *I can resist anything but*. He slips from thought to thought. Wilde Wild Wildness does surely attract him although what he knows about it is not much. Knows (with the oxen) that they prefer common gorse to willow shoots and can balance the topheaviness of their bodies by plaiting their feet as they walk. While with Sad he knows don't mention warplay. Funny word warplay. Never says war or warfare.

I've seen a lot of warplay he'd say. Warplay had me pumped those years. Tip of the spear. Flipswitch inside. She hit the ground 75 saw the white bag 75 bullets tore her head off I saw her hand. I wasn't going to tell anyone back home about. Oh it found its way out it surfaced. I had a tan when I came home no wounds no cuts. Everyone kissed me. Sure I sat by the fire I talked to the old man. There were the smells. The bone beneath. Sweat broke out on me at breakfast. I didn't expect to come home that was not in the plan. Some point I guess the brain cells just give out. You read a hundred military manuals you won't find the word kill they trick you into killing. You get over it it's ok. You have to. Fear not tolerated. Take you out back and shoot you they say. Her eyeglasses in the grass. Standard questionnaire. Fine just say fine. Numb yourself. Wire-frame. Does it feel good at first yes. Play. Guns. Fire. Animals. You know the Carthaginians liked to use oxen for night fighting. I'm talking about Hannibal I'm talking about the battle of Ager Falernus 217 BC. Like tanks but more frightening. They'd tie lit torches to the horns and stampede them toward the enemy. The Romans panicked some ran into the herd some got knocked off the path to the crags below others tried to retreat and were lost in the tundra never seen again. But what about I'm asking what happens when the torches burn down to the horn to the hair to the head to the bone beneath. So much human cruelty is simply incidental is simply brainless. Simply no common sense. You could take the entirety of the common sense of humans and put it in the palm of your hand and *still have room for your dick.*

IT WASHES HER up from the bottom. Slow fluids of dark slide past each other at different speeds. Light she ignores. Waking is gradual lines of dark into sounds. They line up. Before they do is a moment of terror happening every day she every day forgets. Dry little sound is a bird's neckbones sifting into place to sing. Its eyes open and widen. Birds with bigger eyes sing first. Rackety every day to hear this every day forgets. A passing snake splits by. Reds leap the clouds in a wind stirring everything tall all the way out over the river and pinwheeling back as the membrane cracks. Open. The heavens are perfect. Perfection sounds round. Good morning good Io. Bird drops its note into the round and round the note goes circling the wall of the world and stops. After stops is a gap she listens down into for someone who comes *takk takk takking* along she hears *takk takk* slow down and eye and hesitate and *takk takk takking* past. Someone insists and someone will hesitate at this hour. With the heavens perfect and all gazes wet and the bird drops another note into the round and round. Coolly every day forget forgetting all but this not the difference between this and winter does she long for it winter. Where waking is. Where two cloven halves of her hooves clocked in ice and blood crisping along arteries at minus twenty-three degrees is a glory to her. Winter exists and winter is never soon enough. Awake.

HELLO hello / please speak to Sergeant First Class
                              Sad But Great /
                              it's the middle of
                              the night may I
                              ask who's

                              calling / I am Lieutenant
                              M'hek / sorry who /
                              warrior transition team of
                              Sergeant Sad / you're the
                              team /

                              small team / you're the
                              guy who comes every
                              evening with the drugs /
                              no   my   team   is
                              nonpsychotropic / so

                              what do you do / talk /
                              does that help him / one
                              test for this question /
                              what test / did he cap
                              himself yesterday /

                              no / did he cap himself
                              today / no / so talk helps /
                              see your point / how we
                              talk how we are allowed
                              to talk is

                              the most part of happy or
                              not / your accent I can't
                              place where are you from /
                              place you never heard of

far far north so far north it
is south [laughs] / your
English is good / thank
BBC / really / really all
night

radio / I'm impressed / I'm
shrewd toiler / what do
you think about Sad /
cannot discuss / ah /
behind his head /

I understand / how about metaphor / okay / if a man is ruined
like a ditch don't keep
washing your hands in

him / say again / sorry poor translation / of what / of old
proverb / ah / well / I'll tell
him you called / tell him

*at the bottom of the ocean
is a layer of water that has
never moved* this I heard
on BBC last night fresh
idea to me / okay will do /
bye

WIFE OF BRAIN

They drank bright mead in cups of gold
They drank bright mead to catch his shrieks
They drank bright mead what kind of knife
They drank bright mead between his cheeks
They drank bright mead was the melody someone sang
You ever see a Pig
In the shape of a man
Shook over hell
And on you went
The teeth it
Shattered the tongue
It rent
You drank bright mead and After bright mead you drank
Nightfall

he thought too dramatic
until the wind rips the
house off the house or so
it seems to him waking.
From a torrent of small
dreams and village guilts
battering the world at full
north across his tossed-
open bed. Naked man in a
state of fact sprawls on the
couch. Help me G calls
out as he dashes to secure
the big double panes
bucking on their hinges.
Snow and ice chunking in.
Sad groans in his sleep.
An iron bar has to fit
through two loops on the
windows. G is forcing it
into place when he thinks
in sudden panic of his
herd. Count the herd first
thing each day. But the
herd is a hundred miles
away in a different
morning dear bolometric
presences and steaming
hides how he longs to put
his hands on them. Io
would slip her horn under
his arm and let him rub
her great hard furred
forehead. Sad thrashes
and slips off the couch.
Fuck. Day glares open.

ANOTHER TOWN

SLAPPED silly by wind it doesn't matter where. Towns are all the same and night more elusive the more north they go. Sad's rules. Night driving. Day sleeping. Ever more north. No tree no bush no barrier no edges or scale just a huge flat hand that sweeps where it will and wrecks what it wrecks. Why didn't I bring Proust. G lays his head on the table it sinks into the table.

A LITTLE ZIPPER whine that runs along the convolutes of his ear licking in under every bone like a bad emotion. It could be morning noon midnight the sound never stops. He stands watching a thousand whitecaps go diagonal on the bay. Components of today include a shape asleep on the floor an erased white world the tumblers vibrating in the closet and he brought the wrong book. Alive in a room as usual.

WEIGHING IT IN his hand he pauses then throws it across the room. Does he hate *Today I Wrote Nothing: The Selected Writings of Daniil Kharms* translated from the Russian by Matvei Yankelevich for some good reason or for not being Proust. Sad is grinding his teeth. G turns on the radio. Think of yourself as a jar says BBC 4. The words are honey. Pour the honey into the jar. G thinks of himself as a jar. It is vaguely sexual. What was it like to feel sexual. To want say this person on the floor. Or any person. Sexual situations yes the haste and ramming yes the hot cold amazing difference between before and after as if a diagram shot inside out he remembers the diagram but the feelings no. Necessity no. One night under the overpass they'd got the sex whiff again. Made a few fumbles. Not enough juice for the squeeze as Sad so neatly put it.

Whose courage? Is anything serious? Daniil Kharms used to lie down on the highway to see if traffic would stop (it did) then walk away. G stands up from the table. He will make his way to the town swimming pool and see what they think of his rather majestic redwinged breaststroke.

GATHERING SWIM GEAR in the bathroom he glances at the mirror. Sharp stab his face no longer young no more beauty impact. Get used to this. Other ways to navigate the world. Did Daniil Kharms have this particular rug pulled out from under him one day in a bathroom in Leningrad it seems unholy to ask. By all accounts a tall striking man who liked to stroll the boulevards in English tweeds and hunting cap. Destitute hungry hounded by the police he wrote *What big cucumbers they sell nowadays!* in a poem about a man who beat another to death with a cucumber during the siege of Leningrad. Miraculous to have a friend like Daniil Kharms a release from causality. But other people's suffering you want to boil it down theorize it historicize it make it go away. G does not like to think of DK lying on the floor of his cell in the psychiatric ward of a Soviet prison hospital far removed from English tweeds from cucumbers from his own body. Far removed from his first wife second wife and several children who presumably also starved to death along with the soldiers and the animals in the zoo. No Jesus to cleanse it or koan to throw it off a bridge no Zeus to blast it to Tartaros. You look at your face your face is old but suffering is older. Sounds from the other room. G slips to the hall and opens the door. Gone swimming he calls back as the wind slams.

CROWS AS BIG as barns rave overhead. Still driving north. Night is a slit all day is white. Panels of torn planet loom and line up one behind the other to the far edge of what eyes can see. Just ice says Sad. He opens a window and sea fog pours in. They are passing a beach. Black chunks of lava pile on tangles of black seawrack. Waves tower and smash. White foam explodes upward. Stop if we see seals says G but Sad appears not to hear.

in blue are his eyes. He loves driving into this emptiness. Place that is nothing else but what it is he says. What do you mean G thinks but doesn't ask. Sad would just repeat it. G would just get mad. Do you believe in explanation? I saw a show on TV says G where a cheetah's chasing a gazelle. They slow down the film just as it overtakes it you see a little claw flick out the wrist. Whose wrist? says Sad. Cheetah's says G. Cheetah trips the gazelle. Lands on it. Eats it. Know your weapon says Sad. They drive on. Past cliffs and ice fog steaming down. Ponies in a circle with noses together and tails blown straight out horizontal to the wind.

DAD AND ME and Spam I ever tell you that story? G says no. They'd pulled off the road to eat. Blow the door off the car fuck says Sad when they try to get out so they stay in the car. Fold back the cover of the roadmap to cut Spam on. G asks if Spam reminds Sad of the army. Sad says no Spam reminds him of home. We used to fish catfish from a muddy lake more of a swamp near our house so one day we're out fishing I'm baiting my line and off the stern goes the can of Spam into the lake – that's our lunch says Dad damned if he doesn't make me dive in there and get it. You're joking. No joke I can still see it go flash down the water and in I go and up I come with a can of Spam and *that* ladies and gentlemen *that is the reason why I am a homosexual today!* G laughs. Sad cuts another slab and looks out at the wind.

SULLEN SKY PADS soak out whitely. Day and night alike. Temperature dropping. Car skidding on its chains. They pass cliffs with white shocks of waterfall down them and swallows soaring in and out holes in the rock. *If the sky were crooked, it wouldn't make it any lower.* G stares at the swallows. To have a friend like that. He still hates the book but is beginning to love the man. DK's face on the cover is pure fury and girl's lips. G briefly pictures himself saving DK's life – swooping low in the window of the state prison hospital with a bowl of steaming soup. Stay just long enough to see the broken eyes shine up at him then be on his way. But the dark fact is no bowl of soup could have sustained Daniil Kharms through the 900 remaining days of the siege of Leningrad and a sudden astonishing quiet descends on the car. They are rounding a corner into a tall narrow gorge between cliffs. Wind is gone. Sound is gone. Or going strangely. He looks up and sees a hundred streams of meltwater plunging down the face of the rock each no more than a hand's breadth across. Each closed in its own pitch. The pitches mingle and do not their straight silver frequencies. But Sad is rummaging under his seat for the map. They told me to watch for this he says. Now I know where we are!

ICE GETS DIRTY light is low. They go round three quick turns and everything begins to intensify. A gleamingness that hurts the eyes without improving visibility. The car rebounding from side to side as it clatters over the ice. What ever happened to your autobiography says Sad you were always fiddling with it in the old days. I gave it up says G. Nothing was happening in my life. They look at one another and start to laugh. Sound comes cannoning off the walls.

but how and where and
why no one says the word
lost. We're going a new
way says Sad as they head
toward what looks like a
big doorway. G has maps
open but in the dimness
cannot read them. The
road stops at a square red
sign IMPASSIBLE. They
don't mean us says Sad
backing up to go round the
sign.

MELTWATER AND DEBRIS slosh alongside. They are descending. It is very quiet. Air pressure changing inside the car and the road dips. Comes a hiss a whiplash groan overhead they duck. Car stops. Nothing. Let's reconnoiter says Sad. As they step out sharp cracks go like guns somewhere above them and Sad recoiling at each sound. There is a creak of vast doors. A rush. More guns. G oddly calm. He is noticing the ice give and give back underfoot like a trampoline. Corner. They round it and the world stands still. Huge ice. A sort of cavern all one color as if squeezed out of a tube. Wow the blue says G. He starts to bounce.

QUIT BOUNCING

FUCK (Sad). Sounds keep backfiring past them in all directions. But now G is staring down the cavern. Something seems to be pressing itself out of a fault in the ice. A humanlike form. Dressed in what could be a silver tuxedo. Shimmers faintly and pauses. Not glancing to either side. An intentness to it. See that says G. See what says Sad. Creak. Rush. Guns. The faint form seeps toward another fault in the ice and is gone. Even amid the cold of the cavern some deeper chill wafts back to G and Sad where they stand.

SAD TOLD ME this story once I'm not sure I believe it but you can judge for yourself. It's about a friend of his who spent some years as a mercenary. One winter the friend's outfit got stuck in a town of North Africa. Pointblank light. Radiantly cold. He had a headache all the time. Walking the beach one morning he met a boy he thought was a girl and they got into a bit of a talk a bit of a way of meeting here and there day by day. F called him Lucky. He was a courtly boy. If they slept on the roof Lucky laid a piece of veil over F's face to keep the wind out of his mouth. During the winter F came to know Lucky's mother too a wide-bodied person who wore a man's workshirt over her clothes and had both breast pockets filled with earth where she was sprouting cucumber seeds. Nice and *chaud* she'd say patting her pockets. She supported herself and the boy by keeping a cow in the back kitchen. For its milk and its urine. Urine? said F. Painter's piss she said meaning the local bad folk art got its signature bright yellow pigments from the urine of cows fed on quince. Sometimes they would all three of them put on her lipstick and head to town for the evening. After a few whiskeys she'd always repeat in English the same verse of the King James Bible and laugh. *Catch us the voxes the quick little voxes.* Her son is studying his nails. He glows at night. The night he dies there are red plush curtains at the door shoved aside. A man of town power comes in looking for Lucky. Talk fades the air falls there's a gash of language from the man and he slaps Lucky twice. F rises the mother rises too placing herself directly in front of F so he cannot move. No one is using their eyes on one another they're waiting for a letter that has already arrived or is it time shifting five beats forward now it is F who suddenly sees a lung dribbling and a gray cry. He sees shadows cast by flesh that shreds on the edges of a wound sees the little sucking sound of edges as they smolder open and the red light of the cardiac cavity that's Lucky dying yet this has not happened yet. It happens. And from that moment F cannot stop seeing five beats ahead of time all the time for the rest of his life. Every minute is foreclosed. His present tense abolished. No tooth he breaks on an olive will ever again be unforeseen. He breaks it anyway.

THE ICE FAULT is a slot in the ice as tall as a man that vanishes back into shadow. A smell of something brisk and incongruous laundry? sunlight? lingers at the entrance. G drops to his knees to peer in. Cold stabs up through his trousers. Sad has retreated to the car and started the engine which echoes monstrously everywhere. Moving out! Sad yells putting the car in reverse.

WAS IT SHACKLETON whose teeth shattered at something-something below zero G once asked his brother (the biochemist) and why. Because teeth are porous and can fill with droplets of water which instantly freeze in subzero conditions. The glacial walls go tapering away from him down the ice fault. He plunges into a world at once solid and dissolved but weirdly shadowless as if without dimension. He is colder than ever in his life. Vein by vein as separate numbnesses. Heart crashing in his chest. Gelid wings clack on his back. He can hear the wings move but they are someone else's wings and his teeth are in pain. Freeze means expand means shatter said his brother. G closes his mouth.

of polar adventure fatigue flooding his body in waves. This wonderful longing to lie down surely he's been walking for years surely he should stop and rest a moment against one of those satiny planes of ice that allure on every side. Cucumbers Shackleton Spam why is everything draining away why this silver ebbing and flowing not quite reaching his brain. He is so tired. Pour the honey into the jar. He dozes. A sudden violent sneeze shatters him in all directions. Oh he says aloud let's not die in the jar and with an effort that seems to rip his spine apart arches his upper back. Stiffened wing muscles pull hard against their roots and move into a lift. Pieces of ice break from the primaries and fall in a shower. Again he strains backward and up against what seem like seams of steel thinking maybe I can't do this but all, all at once the coverts jolt terribly free and the motion begins. He is rising. Air grabs his knees. Out of black nothing into perfect expectancy – flying has always given him this sensation of hope – like glimpsing a lake through trees or that first steep velvet moment the opera curtains part – he is keening down the ice fault. Soul fresh. Wings wildawake. Front body alive in a rush of freezing air. He opens his mouth in a cry as red sadness pours away behind him and the ancient smell of ice floods every corner of his skull.

WHY BIRDS HAVE no arms–if you are human you fly with arms straight out in front and horizontal to the ground. To give least resistance. Of course it's exhausting. Don't fight it just do it says G to his arms. He visualizes little pistons all over pumping him forward and this helps for a while but the ache is spreading from his spine in every direction. Down the ice fault pours a steady cold channel of headwind against him. He knows he is slowing and probably looks ridiculous. Am I turning into one of those old guys in a ponytail and wings he thinks sadly. Something skims his cheek. He waves at it vaguely. Predators. His heart sinks. People talk of eagles with a wingspan of 3 meters in the northern regions. He begins to imagine his own heroic death as told by Daniil Kharms. *If the sky* – but now the air is darkening around him and strange vectors dive whizz swoop – he gasps suddenly realizing what it is. Not predators. Ice bats! They are blueblack. They are absolutely silent. They are the size of toasters. And they are drafting him down the ice fault with eerie gentle purpose. A spearhead in front and a convoy each side. His shoulders begin to relax. Is there an etiquette for this he should worry about? Theoretically he can gain 35% efficiency by riding their wheels a while. But it should be some sort of exchange. On the other hand theirs is a volunteer intervention and they do look tireless despite all going so fast there's a smell of burning — he is thinking this odd this smell of burning when the whole mass of them veers around an ice bend and arrives in a vast garage.

ICE BATS GO nimbly
and can stop on a dime.
Here's how you stop. Flap
both wings downward
creating a vortex above
the leading edge of each
wing this allows you to
hover. Then flap once
upward to release suction
as you glide from the
flight path in an attitude of
careless royalty and
subside onto some ledge
or throne with neatly
folded fingerbones. G's
descent is less fine. He
slams into the
blueblackness ahead of
him not expecting it to
stop. Or instantly
disperse. Each bat goes
whizzing its way into an
aperture in the back wall.
BATCATRAZ says a sign
nailed up there. G drops
to the ice floor stunned.
Clever of you to come in
the back way says a voice.
G looks up.

A SPARKING TOOL in one hand indicates he is soldering something. The man is wearing grease-stained overalls. You're looking for the clinic he says pushing up his goggles. G notices a car hoisted aloft behind him. Not that I know of says G.

bring Sad around the
bend. He jolts the car to a
halt and climbs out. You
open today? Replace my
drive shaft? to the man in
overalls who gives Sad a
moment of study. Then
turns to stow his tool.
Dandy he says. Let's hoist
her up and take a look.

it was years ago and Sad's name wasn't Sad yet. First comet. G had just stumbled off a bus they looked at one another and that lasted until G was almost twenty but he. Well. Being a loyal soul himself. Sad's need to make friends everywhere. Sex friends club friends gym friends dope friends shopping friends breakdown friends a common enough problem. Sad didn't see a problem. One day he looked around and G was gone. The farewell letter erased and rewritten so many times it tore through the paper. *Tearstained laughter* a phrase G blushes to remember. *Talking is like drowning* etc. He had laid the letter on the kitchen counter. Moved it. Moved it back. Quiet ticking kitchen. It was the middle of the day. Middle of the world. *Let's get this bandage off quick.* He went over the letter in his mind afterward for months imagining Sad reading it

Sad pierced by it Sad racing down the street with it in his hand. This letter that in fact fell down behind the sink and wasn't found till two years later by some friend of Sad's who fished it out and started to read it aloud – to his credit Sad stopped him. Anyway the driveshaft proving uncooperative they break for a cup of tea. The man in overalls has an office in the clinic behind the garage and a lab coat on a peg by the door. He changes from overalls to lab coat. *CMO* says the lapel in gold cursive. He sees G looking at this. I just fix cars for fun he says and laughs an uneven laugh. What's a CMO thinks G but doesn't ask. They follow into a sort of lobby. And there in the morbid light is a tall dazzled man who sweeps onto Sad saying I knew you would come.

WIFE OF BRAIN

first reversal they've come
by mistake to a private clinic beside a glacial lake run
by a guy in overalls who (luckily) does know how to install
a driveshaft although he
just laughs when
they ask how

long it will take "reversal" because
the short road trip Sad
had in mind is soon to be redefined
by one who calls himself
a god and is

arguably no fake "reversal" because little snags come tumbling
out of the text like what's it like
to be a prophet (a 4NO) and would you decide
to
act your age
if you really could see what's next

YOU SPELL IT number 4
letter *N* letter *O* no space
all caps: 4NO / is it a
nickname / no Babycakes
it's functional the fucking

army being a fucking
fulcrum of fucking
functionality / they called
you 4NO in the army / are

you going to repeat
everything I say / sorry
/ pass the sugar / so you
knew Sad in the army /
indeed I did / he

says you can see the future
you're a prophet / no I see
Seeing I am the god of this
I see Seeing coming /

what's that like / all white
all the time / what do you
mean / I mean the whole
immediate Visible crushed

onto the frontal cortex is
nothing but white without
any Remainder now you'll
say of course there's no

Remainder if a thing hasn't
happened yet! but the
fact is most of what you

people see most of what you

people call the present world is just Remainder just a failure of Invisibility's flames to disappear from that

thin edge / a failure / they were always coming up to me saying 4NO who'll win the hockey pool 4NO your

name means Foresight better get some 4NO you're the god who knows the future how come you got yourself

fuckstuck in this meatclock didn't you see it coming / well didn't you / what I saw coming was the atomic

essence of the Visible brought to such a density its Incandescence left no place for anyfuckingthing else /

ah / or am I talking outside your experiential zipcode / sort of / give me that sugar again / so this white stuff's

coming at you all the time
/ yup / you can't stop it / I
can slow it down with
alcohol or pharmaceuticals
I

choose not to / was it
different in the army / hell
yes we were drugged to
the eyeballs / Sad doesn't
talk about

that much / no I bet not /
well   he   mentioned
something at a crossroads
/ say again / a crossroads a

woman a shopping bag a
white plastic bag I don't
know / here's some advice
/ yes / don't ask about the

woman don't ask about the
crossroads don't ask about
the plastic shopping bag /
okay / don't ask him don't

ask me / okay / time for
my meds I'll leave you
now / it was a pleasure /
oh I doubt that

WIFE OF BRAIN

4-B Ration
24-Hour Ration
Battle Ration
Combat Ration
boiled sweets
Combat Ration for One Man
Combat Ration for Five Man
Field Ration
First Strike Ration
Garrison Ration
Individual Food Ration
do you ever think about Bakelite closures bronze amphoras
portion control
about pallet loads purifying tablets dried fish
Individual Meal Pack
Instant Meal Individual
Jungle Ration
Main Battle Tank Ration
Meal Ready to Eat
One Man Compo Pack Ration
One Person Pack
a plastic spoon wrapped in a napkin
Operational Ration Pack General Purpose
Patrol Ration One Man
Self-Defense Portion
lemon/orange powder known as "screech"
Special Forces Ration
Special Fighting Ration
you're hungry or maybe you're not hungry maybe you're just
irritable
Survival Kit
a 400-g can of rice

TWELVE FOIL PACKETS arranged on each tray in three rows of four. *Ration* is a beautiful word or so the CMO thinks. Key to a disciplined life. Latin *ratio* "reason." Rationality. Principle of order. A prescribed amount at a prescribed time. It's how you keep animals in line it works for people too he says. Please sit. Gesturing to his guests he takes the chair at the head of the table. They sit. They are clients of his kingdom and clients like to be entertained in his spotless cafeteria. Each place around the table is set with an identical aluminum tray. Sad is staring at his tray with unnatural focus. 4NO leans toward him. Nostalgia Sad? Those unforgettable MREs? Don't eat the Lucky Charms! He laughs horribly. Sad looks at him with eyes gone inside out and heaves to his feet toppling his chair. Exits. Is there a problem? says the CMO tearing open the perforated corner of a packet of mackerel in olive oil. Too much memory is the problem says 4NO. We had to look at a fuck of a lot of these little foil packets in the army. Weird you got 'em here too. Don't bother me anymore. Course I never ate the Lucky Charms. Horrible laugh.

Charms what does that mean? says G. Means don't fuck with outcomes says 4NO. Means a meal ration in the army always has a pack of Lucky Charms. Nobody ever ate 'em. Obvious reason. Except one day Sad decides he don't need lucky he has charms of his own and charm to spare. He ate his. What happened? says G. Well that my boy you'll have to get from the superhero himself. Ain't my give. The CMO is tucking into his oat biscuit and cherry puree. Words can kill he says with his mouth full. Look at Oedipus. G looks at the CMO. You're saying Lucky Charms carry an ancestral curse. The CMO wipes his lips with a napkin. I'm saying if the army is issuing your Luck in the form of Charms it's already gone. 4NO hoots once and gets up from the table. You gentlemen are wading too deep for me this evening I'm out. He takes his tray and goes. So you let people eat in their room says G. No actually not says the CMO. Smiles. I'll have to remind him. He's a patient right says G but you treat him special. The CMO is studying his strawberry beverage packet. Let's say 4NO has a need to break rules. Of course he wouldn't put it that way he'd say he sees an aberrant future where that particular rule is not in force. So you don't believe in his prophetic ability says G. The CMO taps the packet against his cheek. Do I think his brain chemistry is unusual yes. Do I credit the *all white all the time* visionary stuff no that's a dodge. What's he dodging says G. Same thing as your friend the superhero. Those pesky traumatic memories. Each of the CMO's eyes has a very still black center. But you don't know much about that do you? he says. No says G not much. That's good then says the CMO. He is smoothing his empty foil packets and organizing them into two stacks on his tray. Shall we go find SBG? He is rising from the table. You're the only one who calls him that you know says G. Acronyms appeal to me says the CMO. Name rations says G. The CMO pauses. Clever. Yes. Name rations. Perhaps I will like you after all.

UP ALL NIGHT feels like a chewed butt. Chairs make him nervous. Knots himself about the room. What jabs in and out of his periphery. *Your movements upset me* no one hears. Closes his eyes. Who is that yelling. Opens a slit. Rec room is empty except for 4NO with arms held wide. *Behold I am Prometheus! O roaring universe that aches and sings! You see me suffer at the hands of gods and I a god!* 4NO is practicing his play. Sad now against a wall he can't remember leaning on. *Bang bang* no one hears. Sleeps tilt inside him all the old stale unslept sleeps of all the years since he looked and he was lost. Lie still at night he could not he cannot. Every flap to be peered under every crevice to be crept into every chustling memory there they go like clockroaches. Memory tore at his father in him and he weeps in a sort of fury turning to the wall he cannot bear people saying this (a sort of fury) people have no idea. What things are like for him physical things this blacker and blacker spiral down it goes. His looks are gone. Strength broken. He hates pity. A current of blacker flows through him. Impairment and he lie down on the floor. Arms throw themselves over himself. Prometheus is still addressing the universe *Where are your eyes? What is your justice? You see me gripping this frayed rope-end of pain for the last ten thousand years! Who will free me finally?* Sad goes blank. Later the floor straightens and hardens around him. Eyes open. But they are breakable. He will not move them. *My heart is like a singing bird.* Does he say this. 4NO has crossed the room and is standing above him. Get your head out of your butt 4NO says nudging a boot. Sad views him upside down. *Whose nest is in a water'd shoot* no one hears. He staggers upright. 4NO starts to hum. They waltz.

MEN WALTZ ELLIPSOIDALLY like balloons G thinks. He is watching from the doorway. Eighteenth-century balloons. He'd gone to an academic dinner (academic boyfriend) once. Cretan archaeology (left) and eighteenth-century balloons (right) the two ancient ladies he was seated between. He paddled the blues of Knossos during the soup course then turned with the haddock to the best part of ballooning is watching your own shadow race over the ground below. Yes! as a winged person he knew the racing self its aureole of mysterious light gathered from dictionaries we no longer use its strange little pathos way down there. She (right) was soon grinning with all her battered teeth and sailing on (past haddock) to "splash and dash" technique also called "flathatting" she ruffled his nape as if they both were boys. Your custard is cooling said Knossos (left). A roar of gravel in the driveway jolts

G from reverie. He glances to the window. Here's Ida climbing from the back of a taxi and the CMO after her. Up the surprised front steps. Her plaid sportscoat looking not so fresh. Dread skips into G. If Ida is here who's looking after the herd?

WIFE OF BRAIN

great illness makes great doctors or so

the CMO tells us

having

waited years for his Warhol

in a clinic full of Valerie

Solanases then a night of deep snow

brought an admit

for

4NO whose theories however balmy are a welcome

change from the reductionist voodoos of psychotherapy that

are a CMO's

bounden duty usually now

watch everyone's mood become quite lopsided

as the spark struck

by Ida flares into doom

provoking

dissension on that old tragic question who are we at the whim

of (whom?) whom

hums the tune

HE KNOWS HER cunning she knows him hungry. He calls himself the CMO she calls him Pig Doc. Tell me Pig Doc she says why I'm always stealing. Because it's the opposite of *feeling* he says. She grins. Silly rhymer. Rhymes don't cure you. Yet it pierces her grid so she closes the grid with others of her own bad deal get real cucumber peel as he goes on. To *feel* anything deranges you. To be seen *feeling* anything strips you naked. In the grip of it pleasure or pain doesn't matter. You think what will they do what new power will they acquire *if they see me naked like this*. If they see you *feeling*. You have no idea *what*. It's not about *them*. To be seen *is* the penalty. You shame victim after victim they are all *you*. Nature is on the *inside*. He sees her looking at the print on the wall behind his desk and switches to Cézanne how naked the apples got in his hands. Saucy jake says Ida. Naked naked naked all you ever say. The doctor is pleased. He's drawn her out he's done a bit of educating he's inserted a few innuendos and this only their second session! Ida is pleased. Her grid intact. Smart grid. Safe lovely shadows chase themselves brainacross in the thin particular light she keeps there. Home light. Watch that grid. You'll tell me if there is anything you need says Pig Doc. His hunger like a smell on him she turns her head away. But here is the holiness of mastery that was taught her by her father. It is to treat your enemy as an honored guest. Get me some paper I'll draw you some naked she says. You want naked. Pig Doc blushes. Their time is up. Exit Ida. *Pursue Cézanne* he notes in his dossier.

LOOKING GOOD IDA / sarcastic don't help / you
abandoned my herd / I
missed you Gerry now
you fussing at me already
/

don't call me Gerry / listen it was here or jail / you
got arrested / you could
say / how / hit up a
laundromat / shit Ida / was
okay except a few details /
details / off-duty cop
happens to be doing his
laundry

/ cop / grabs my gun throws it in the dryer / gun /
where it melted / your gun
melted / was plastic / I'm
picturing this / I found it
under the overpass
anyway here's the thing /
I'm listening / attempted
armed

robbery could be jailbars for Ida so Ida puts on her
thinking cap / you made a
deal / deal what deal
what's Ida put up in a deal
/ good question / no I did a
bit of bipolar / you faked
psychosis / bluedog
blackbile hissy

fit I did yes I went down the checklist / this was in
the courtroom / backseat

/ what backseat / backseat
of the

cop car where the cop's dryhumping me on the way
to the station / shit Ida /
and since I knew you guys

is here / back up now just first tell me what about the
herd / M'hek got 'em / who
/ Lieutenant M'hek that
guy

from Sad's unit / you gave my herd to a total stranger
/ M'hek can handle it / Ida
tell me this isn't true / quit

hollering / I'm not hollering / your head's on fire / so
what happens next / eyes
pop out eyebrows sizzle
off / I mean with the herd /
M'hek'll phone you
tomorrow the next day /
oh fine / Gerry I done my
best in a difficult situation
/ I can't believe you gave
my herd away difficult
situation shit! and what do
you mean you knew we
were here nobody knew
we were here / so how's
Sad / it was pure

chance we came here nobody knew / but how is he
really / can't believe
you're frolicking in
laundromats while my

                    herd goes to total strangers
                    / what's a hole made of
                    Gerr / is this a riddle

/ no / itself a hole's made of itself / I think so too /
                    and don't call me Gerr /
                    got it

THE LONG BODY is always a surprise. The actual touching neither a positive nor a negative experience they each would admit but no one does. A new tract of nature is open. No one wants to set foot first. So after sex they talk about the weather up north which they dislike and exchange advice. Sad tells her how to get traction on glare ice (pour Javex down your tires) she tells him how to find a sunk dead body in a lake or river (float a loaf of bread down the current). Loaf of bread will stop over the body she says. Meanwhile in another room of the clinic G is dreaming of Daniil Kharms. They are driving along in a paper car. G has a big roll of newsprint which he is cutting into stretches of road and leaning out to toss them in front of the car. This is hard to do from the passenger seat and Daniil Kharms has to keep swerving the car to stay on

the road. Is he getting fed
up? G worries. Daniil
Kharms turns to him. Cut
me an incognito he says.
G goes white with shame.
He hadn't even thought of
this! Daniil Kharms could
have been saved! He sits
up suddenly drenched in
ringing. Phone.

HELLO Hello M'hek here / don't you ever sleep /
herd report / what's wrong
with the herd / nothing
wrong with the

herd / you sure / absolutely / everyone eating / eating
well / everyone shitting /
shitting well / no parasites
/

no sign of a parasite / how's the mood / Io is sad / but
coping / coping well / this
is better than I expected /

M'hek is efficient in small matters / I owe you M'hek
/ new topic / go ahead /
our mutual friend the
Sergeant Sad /

yes / supposed to be calling in every 72 hours / ah /
we suggest he rectify / I'll
pass it along / our faith is
in you

/ he's a mess these days / cannot discuss / he's
drinking again / how about
a proverb / shoot / if the
reverse side

has no reverse side keep eyes front / too late for that
one / do your best /
goodnight Lieutenant /
over and out

A CERTAIN CLICK of certain doors in certain corridors. The Laundry Room door. Certain midnights. It is directly underneath the room where he sleeps or doesn't. Rigid in the bed he bites down on the sound. On the gap after. His ears tangle in it. Sexual jealousy? Not exactly. But comparison is involved. Comparison makes you less interesting to yourself doesn't it. Your magic contracts your body putting forth no frill under another's gaze. Ida wears the frill now. He wonders how Ida finds Sad as a lover. He wonders if she lies watching moonlight ease its way among the washing tubs the hampers the gallons of bleach lined up on the shelf. Men fall asleep straight after sex and girls get used to it. G never did. The moonlit ironing boards grandstanding like steeds.

in fact. Ida is watching the room itself. It looks lonely a room needs its work. Once as a child she'd stayed in a department store overnight just to see. She stole nothing. She wanted to understand the way it was with no one watching. She'd brought her drawing book but found it hard to do anything in the dark. She sucks her fingers. His smoky aftertaste. What was it like? he asked after the first sex. Like pie without a fork she said. He smiled. I know about the fork he said. That was their closest moment. It inspired her to step past fear. To believe she had got outside the circle of her mistakes. But then he said you know Ida I'm a man who doesn't like the idea of being liked too much and another night he said love was a big bunch of grass that grows up in your mind and makes you stupid. So much for pie. She leans on her elbow watching Sad and wishing she had her drawing book with her. They are lying on a pile of mattress covers on the floor in weak light from somewhere a night that could so easily not exist. Drawings of Sad so far are minimal. She'd looked at the photos in his wallet and copied one of his father taken the day he dropped his eyeglasses down the well. In the photo he looks younger than Sad is now this father who refused to get another pair of glasses because *I was already seeing too much*. Ida wants to meet the father. Sad is making groaning sounds in his sleep. She touches him. Night's bones are still forming. They get up stiffly and crowd into their clothes and grope across to the big door. Slip out. There against the wall of the corridor sits G with his knees up. Howdy says G.

THINKING ABOUT PROUST to pass the time. What a scamp that Proust. That Albertine. Does anyone really believe the girl stays asleep for four pages in volume V while Marcel roams around her prostrate form and stretches out beside it on the bed. He touches her lips strokes her cheek presses his leg to her leg then spends a long time staring at the kimono flung on a chair with all her letters in the inside pocket. *Albertine continuait de dormir.* He says he likes her better asleep because she loses her humanity and is just a plant. A sleep plant that cannot tell him lies or escape his knowing. Poor Marcel. What is there to know.

WITH RED PENCIL G had underlined the sentence where Proust observes the momentarily impaired surface of the eye of a person who has just had a thought she will not tell you. It traces a fissure in the pupil and disappears back down its own involuntary depths. Watch the wake.

LIES WHITE LIES half-lies combinations of lies degrees of improbability that lead up to and away from an outright lie these layer themselves in the archaeology of Albertine's answers to simple questions. *L'après-midi d'Albertine* this lost city whose smashed clues and indecipherable evidence poor Marcel has to dig through each evening feverish for a real shard. How was your day? this question on which so much hangs. You don't really want to know. Yet he keeps digging. G could never bear to watch Sad sleep.

YOU LOOK THIN you losing weight? says Sad to G and starts to cry. The Laundry Room door closes gravely behind him. G had a thousand things to say but they vanish. Let's keep it quiet whispers Ida. They stare at one another all three of them wanting to grasp this moment where they are crowded like frozen travelers around a stove. Wanting a tiny burnished world and for a moment they glimpse it. Sad turns away.

swaying off down the corridor. Organize my life. G sinks his head onto his knees. Ida studies the corridor. Dark matter she thinks. Telescopes can't focus it scientists can't say what it is but it weighs more than everything we see put together. She heard a dark matter expert on the radio one day now it makes sense. The corridor is full of it. She sits down beside G.

A SALMON ANSWERS

Ida when G asks. Some conversations are not about what they're about. The word *conversation* means "turn together." Turn a salmon turn home turn Prometheus a hopeful god. Turn organize his life! Do not turn betrayal not kiss. Night bones. Day sleeper. Girl. Not stark naked not stark itself. What do you want to be in your next life. A salmon. Why. A rescue. How. A play. Whose. A reading. When. A Friday. No. Is that why they call it the Rec room.

DO NOT TURN his photographs he had them out the other day spread all over the floor I said who cut out the faces. He said I can't sleep I can't remember what to think about when I'm sleeping I said why think just sleep. He said I found her bloody eyeglasses in the grass after nothing else was left not even. Not even what I said. Not even the stupidfuck white plastic shopping nothing her family could. Bury identify keep turn. One lens smashed the other. Why cut I said he said they needed more shadow. Okay. The other okay. The other okay.

WIFE OF BRAIN

tears differ you know
some
people cry in the wind
others in sorrow
emotional tears having
in them high
concentrations of
manganese which irritant
tears lack all those bowls
of secret milk he weeps
easily we
simply note this oh
his Dad had hopes a little
warplay
might straighten stiffen
darken whatever
that yelp of his
to something like
backbone but watch him
go crawling
plank to plank
and the big Zeus eye
drilling his every noon
hello torn soul is too
easy to say here's the
picture he falls through the
picture eventually
he
has to climb back up
it is the Climbing that exists

ITS ENTIRE FUTURE
jumps into his eyes.
Rooms always startle him.
Doorways. The
bronzeclad heroes of
Homer had a better idea.
To stand in time with your
back to the future your
face to the past what a
relief it would be 4NO
thinks. Homer doesn't
mean that literally says the
CMO whenever they talk
about this. Two prep
school boys quibbling
over Homer except 4NO
often ends up calling the
CMO a 10-gallon asshat.
This plays well on TV.
Originally he agreed to do
the talk shows to please
the CMO and pay off his
bill at the clinic but has
come to like TV and TV
hosts with their
syncopated eyes and same
questions. What is it like
to be a prophet etc. etc.
Audiences like him too –
tall and scatological and
doesn't care if he makes
sense. He gradually
realized he could just rant.
It was like angry
sleepwalking. But today
things are different.

Today he very much wants to hear the words of his play rise and shine in a roomful of people. He very much wants to be awake for this. He will read all the parts himself and now elides other thought. The reading is scheduled for 5 o'clock. He begins to set up the chairs.

CHAIRS BLUE (20) for inmates. Chairs gray (10) for visitors. Chairs reserved (8) for the CMO. Place for Sad to lie down. Pots and pans for the musical accompaniment (Ida's idea) but where are these? He looks around frowning. Enter Ida. Forgot the pots she says and turns to go back. Wait a minute take this. He holds out a big white plastic bag. You know where to go? Kitchen's in the basement past the Laundry Room and down that hall. Get everything they'll let you have he says. Exit Ida. 4NO closes his eyes. Elides the jab of worry. Starts doing his stretches.

IDA IN THAT doorway is a moment many will be changed by but she doesn't return to the doorway for a long time. What is it about basements. Ida often gets lost in basements well in fact Ida often gets lost. Despite map or compass. Spaces change shape on her nothing matches chunks fall out the back of a real day. *You'll Never Be Lost Again: The Complete Guide to Improving Your Sense of Direction* a book on sale in supermarkets was helpful through Chapter 1 ("You Are Here") and Chapter 2 ("Tools and Attitude") but turned frightening in Chapter 3 which posed the question Why does a mirror reverse your image from L to R but not top to bottom? not front to back? Approaching mirrors sideways she would hope and not hope to surprise the back of her head. Studying *You'll Never*'s diagrams made a sensible crease not quite a pain in her brain. Chapter 4 ("Mental Rotation of a Three Dimensional Object") featured small black & white sketches of bricks piled in unlikely ways and labeled A, B, C. They were the tidiest of drawings. She stared hard at them and felt more and more wrong. Something bleak about the bricks reminded her of Christmas at home. She put the book away. So when 4NO gives her the plastic bag and she turns from the doorway her nerves are already tingling. On her way to the kitchen she cleverly follows a guy going down and arrives without thinking as fast as a hole dug in sand. *Without thinking* was a key error she realizes as she starts back. *You'll Never* had emphasized being observant on the outbound journey. Also take your time and do not panic. Also bring neon zip ties and tie them to branches high up. She shifts the plastic bag now

heavy with pots and pans
to her other hand.
Corridors branch dimly
around her. The familiar
Laundry Room nowhere
in sight.

I AM VERY he says tilting into the room and stops. Happy to see you man but I'm not sure you're real. Tell me you're real. 4NO looks at him upside down then unfolds from his headstand. Bad night? says 4NO. But Sad is straying about the room touching all the chairs one by one. Chairs he says. I missed you. His voice is soft. His eyes drift off. 4NO watches him fragilely. Every molecule of Sad and Sad's bad future is advancing through 4NO's retinal surface. Like perfect works of art they form a sparkling flood. They saturate him and confiscate the present moment. He closes his eyes against this unbearable excess and gathers his mind to a point. It breaks through the white. He opens his eyes. At ease soldier he says to Sad. Nobody's here yet. I'm just stretching. Sad smiles and then forgets not to. The smile stays on his face.

JUST HOT MILK on the curb here Ida says Ida. Let's move. She hoists the plastic bag and sets off in some direction. Takes a corner. Keeps going. Down a long hall. Through a swing door. Round another bend. Reckless now. Skin electric. This takes centuries. All of a sudden there is a man in a silver tuxedo ahead of her walking rather fast. A smell of fresh wind or laundry in his wake. She calls out speeds up. He has a tight intent motion like a bail bondsman hurrying to court. They round a corner together. Go up some stairs. Is he familiar? His silver tux gives off a sheen in the cellar dusk. He is not slowing down. Centuries. Ida feels a rise of irritation and is about to call out again when they take a last turn he vanishes. She has arrived in the open doorway of the Rec room and her bag of utensils slams her leg as she comes

to a halt. The room is full
of people who turn to her.

A STARTLED STICK in a plaid sportscoat is what some see. Ida in the doorway. Others confused by the plastic bag think of groceries and miss their life at home. A few assume the play has started and this is the protagonist. The CMO fails to see her at all he is shaking hands most of the donors busy with their phones don't look up. The woman who suffers from dementia and whose habit is to repeat the words *Away   Away   Away* unceasingly ceases. The man who trembles and cannot close his eyelids all the way even at night says *What a charmer* in tones of pure delight because he hasn't slept for years and this alters your reaction to simple   sights.   The trembling man will be important for Sad who at this moment is staring at Ida and seeing the most grievous day of his life rematerialize before him nor will it come one more grievous the wave of war

bearing him along the
sound of his rounds going
out trigger breaking crisp
in his finger.

THAT BLACK PERIPHERAL motion is Sad hurtling past 4NO toward Ida and would have knocked her flat and broke her bones had the trembling man not launched himself in between just in time. The room falls apart. Ida still upright her pots and pans flying. People yell and run. *Away Away Away* starts up again on a panic note. It's that white plastic bag (4NO to himself) why didn't I think. Why didn't I think.

ONCE UPON A time (according to myth) each person was born with an exact knowledge of the day and hour of their own death. Poor souls could think of nothing else. They lived breathless with terror. Then Prometheus arrived bringing with him the amazing gift that is the subject of 4NO's play. A roomful of people ready for *Prometheus* now gaze astonished at the trembling man tackling Sad in the doorway even as Ida bursts into song.

                    chorus
                    should we discuss your
                    philanthropy
                    prometheus
                    I went a bit too far
                    chorus
                    how do you mean
prometheus
I stopped them seeing death before them
                    chorus
                              who
                    prometheus
                    human beings
                    chorus
                    how
prometheus
I planted blind hope in their hearts
chorus
why
                    prometheus
                    they were breaking
                    chorus
                    you fool

                    from 4NO's *Prometheus
                    Rebound*

WHAT IS A culture? A culture is what approves or disapproves of the actions in its midst. Yet how rare for approval to be unanimous. Ida's instinct to sing is right on the money. She ionizes the room as a Taoist rainmaker raises his voice to the clouds at the very moment the dragons come charging out. All sing. Patients sing. Nurses sing. Kitchen staff sings. Even the donors sing. Numb normal vanishes. Hopes float free – macaroni for supper let the catheter not slip true love new meds play the cello again –

AND YET HOPE turns out to be let's face it mostly delusion a word derived from Latin *ludere* meaning "to play a game with oneself or with others" or so the CMO finds himself explaining at the press conference next day amid a long obfuscating response to the reporter's question How did the riot get started? It was a misunderstanding he finally sums up. Was the vet holding a gun? No he was just playing around. But someone got hurt? One of our elderly patients struck his head falling. You killed a patient? He was already frail it may have been a seizure an autopsy is scheduled. And the woman? Ida is fine. The video clip you authorize that? know the chiclet could sing? know she could kick? Here the CMO withdraws from comment. A video clip of Ida in the doorway leading the whole room in song is indeed circulating in local and nonlocal media outlets. But those minutes of fame bring Ida little joy. Her main memory of the doorway is Sad lunging up from the floor to come at her with murder in his black eyes. Sad full of hate. Sad as a stranger. She kickboxed him flat and kept singing.

PLOWING CAN BE
brutal. So too hauling. Io
prefers ambling. Ahead of
the herd at her usual pace in
her usual leadership role on
their usual way to summer
pasture. Not summer yet
but here they go. That's not
usual. M'hek walks slightly
behind her. He's not usual.
The wind is from the north.
Usual. Her head itches.
Usual. She stops and
lowers her head to scrape
one horn against a patch of
gorse. The gorse smells
interesting. She bites off
some and stands a while
working it against her
mostly toothless upper jaw.
Especially pungent this
gorse. It is half-fermented
and will cause her mild
hallucinations all the rest of
the day. Or perhaps not so
mild.

WIFE OF BRAIN

what is the difference between
poetry and prose you know the old analogies prose
is a house poetry a man in flames running
quite fast through it
or
when it meets the mind waves appear (poetry) or
both are defined by
length of lines *and there are times*
your life gets like that whispers
Ida gets like
what? says the news anchor
leaning to peer in Ida's telegenic face but Ida
says nothing like Andy
(speaking of telegenic)
Warhol she's
cool with
letting TV take her for a liar
or a
fool

YOU WANT TRUTH you get it from somebody who wore the shoe Ida says to the blond TV anchor who comes poking the day after the riot! *Riot!* being the TV word for what happened in the Rec room that day instead of 4NO's play. Tears pour in Ida's heart but not her eyes as she sits calmly answering questions about daily life at the clinic. The TV person is rather out of breath. How to draw that.

THEY ESCAPE SAME
night with Sad in a suicide
suit they can't untie so
they bundle him into the
car as such. No one has
much to say. The road
glows whitish blue.
Behind them the glacier
diminishes. Close to
dawn 4NO driving. Do
you know the way? says G
from the backseat. Let's
say I can see us getting
there says 4NO. That's
not the same thing is it?
You want to drive you can
drive. G retreats into
silence. They are
speeding along the
seacoast. The sea has a
paralyzed black sheen.
Now and again Sad
collapses forward in a
narcotic heap G shoves
him back onto the
cushions. Who are these
transparent people? Sad
wonders then sleeps again.
Ida in the front passenger
seat does not turn around.

LAID HIS SNOUT on her. Cold and wet and sliding it keeps replaying in her mind. Their final session. He made clear her usefulness to him. Her future as a clinic celebrity. A series of mini-documentaries a producer a brand name. His snout on her wrist the purposiveness the wet cold slidingness of it or was it a sort of oblivion in him made her pivot and let fly a kick to his windpipe that knocked him out the door of his office and down the hall despite the awkward angle. How satisfactorily it bookended the kick to Sad's throat that began this little event horizon. But now she feels a bit lost. Her father taught her to kick when she was ten. What would he think of her current trend? Would he give her his *Ida don't be glad of yourself* look? He'd died by mistake when they took him to the ER for measles and some distracted doctor put him in a room with a scarlet fever. You got a technicality there *you could sue those fuckers blind* so people said to Ida and her mother at the funeral but who had the heart. She tries to remember his low voice. When they practiced together he could adjust her form with the slightest nudge. How about this? he'd so quietly murmur moving her elbow a centimeter to the left and the energy shot down her arm like lightning. She can feel the shapes of it still in her body and her timing. How sweet if she could hear his voice again just once. But something is catching at the corner of her eye. Glances out the window sees a man in a silver tuxedo loping alongside the car with his eyes intent on the horizon and a shine around him like washed air. She rolls down the window. A bright smell streams into the car. Doesn't she know this man? She puts this away to think later and leans her head out. Need a lift?

WHERE YOU headed /
bit further along the road /
why

you running / oh I often do
/ are you

meeting someone / yes
/ who / a stranger / how
will

you recognize each other /
in a strange way / strange

to both of you / that

would have been a
problem / it's no longer a
problem / no

WITH HERMES IN the car everything changes. They don't know it is Hermes. Don't know they are headed for death. Except 4NO in the driver's seat is experiencing an exceptionally high photon count and consequent fatigue of his visual cortex. Sad wakes up. Ida turns around. They smile at each other a smile that dazzles the car. G feels such a stab of envy plus love plus hate he laughs aloud. Then cries What's that red up ahead?

SMILE FROM INSIDE

(him) this one jostled alert by G shifting over to make room for the man in the silver tuxedo. The pressure of G along his right side brings a snow of memories cascading all the old joys run up and down his limbs once. A woman whom he does not know is turning to him from the front seat. Her teeth are spectacular. She bares them like a lioness come down to the pool to drink. He has worked his hands free from their restraints and thinks to throttle the lioness. But maybe he does know her. He pauses. Someone is yelling. Sorry he says was that me yelling.

SMILE FROM INSIDE
(her) is pure bravura.

Wife of Brain

don't say you weren't
expecting a volcano those
red wings
that not even bad love can
tame
must signify something's
somewhere
about to go up in flame or
(as Proust says) be
eternalized in pleasure
like the men
in a Pompeian house of ill
fame yet fame
is not ill
for all
in this tale Sad may be a
goner
but Io's getting ready
for her free
throw
with one eye on the herd
and the other on that
pyroclastic glow

EACH SEED AS he crushes it in his teeth shoots a suds of sharp red cream along his tongue. M'hek is eating a pomegranate in the dark. He avoids its bitter membrane jacking out the seeds one by one with the point of a knife. His beard and hands are stained. A thin wild fragrance rises on the air this interests Io in a psychedelic way. She is still high on fermented gorse and ambles over to where he sits crosslegged on the ground. The rest of the herd is asleep in a patch of saxifrage. She studies M'hek and with a long slow blink of her deepshaded golden eyes extends her tongue. No one can know what another's ecstasy is and yet when M'hek wipes four pomegranate seeds off his knife blade onto the blackish groove of Io's tongue she shivers all over. Here is a taste for every bud M'hek thinks. Io subsides slowly and gigantically to the ground. Together they inhale the

first blue of day as it starts
seeping out of hills all
around. Io leans her
horn against M'hek's knee.
A hush carries itself up
her sigh. Late stars watch
them.

certain others in the same night. Evacuation procedures are under way at the clinic. Despite various vulcanologists giving him various predictions about timing and direction of lava flow the CMO knows when the bats depart Batcatraz is time to go. First he scours 4NO's room and finds all 4NO's notes for the play and takes them. Ida's room looks clean as a whistle. He ponders this expression while searching her cupboards and mattress. Of course she took her drawing book with her. Nothing clean about a whistle. She came whistling through this late season of his life. He had reached winter without discontent had learned to feel at home in his human costume. Poor lamb what costume could survive Ida. A person without imposture and for all her illegalities an enemy of misrule. A person who extrudes her own soul before her as she goes. Like lava. He laughs unevenly. The defection of the four of them has not surprised him and he knows he will make use of it somehow. But a large chunk of his gossip life is gone and he needs gossip it keeps him dynamic. He is a person always in motion he needs to be kept vibrating. Between any two activities he plunges. Can't stand to be alone hates quiet time has little interest in introspection let alone other people as individuals. Or rather he doesn't care for people he cares what flows through them. And usually takes it. His teacher at med school called him a minotaur who swallows other people's labyrinths. Good I'll do psychiatry he said.

really were tedious as it turned out. He would have gone back to fixing cars except for 4NO. What a godsend was 4NO with his Promethean pretensions and meaty complaints about *all white all the time.* The man never stopped sparking and changing you could plug your battery into 4NO and run for a year. What is it like to be a prophet? The CMO usually pretends to doubt 4NO's foreknowing but the fact is he does not understand it. Clearly the man lives in a different mental world than other people and the difference is not a matter of predicting who'll win the World Cup. 4NO seems to foresee about five seconds ahead of every instant. Do prophets vary in their amplitude of vision? Maybe Isaiah had an oscillating variable of forty years or a century. Five seconds gives you 4NO. Either way is a mess – you have no present moment not skinned shaved stained saturated overrun outraged by raw data from the future. Never a moment of naked eye. 4NO functions pretty well considering.

BETTER THAN ISAIAH the CMO thinks. Isaiah was too emotional. 4NO plays his cards close to his chest. It's true he slips into a rant from time to time but in general there's a cool control that the CMO assumes was trained into him in the army. What was the army like for 4NO? He does not seem to be lashed to fury whenever he remembers it (like Sad) although now and again he tells stories that make people simply turn away. And does so with a kind of exasperation as if to say Oh you've a ways to go but soon enough you'd be stomping infant skulls and see the sport of it *you'd get there too*. The CMO looks out the window. A crude black wasteland smell is invading Ida's room. Lava two miles away at a guess. He expedites his search. Makes a minor but puzzling discovery. A wad of fliers from some martial arts academy tied up in rubber bands. He briefly pictures Ida on a streetcorner pressing leaflets into passing hands. Rejects the picture. Takes the fliers anyway. You could never learn enough about Ida.

IO IS AWARE of the volcano well before M'hek. She lifts her head and looks back at the herd. It is shambling to its feet. Eyes gone black and absolute. Sweat sour as a schizophrenic. M'hek decides they should move out. The herd is averse it balks and drifts. Io cooperates doubtfully. Finally they set off. About a half mile up the road they arrive at a cliff edge and all simply stop. M'hek looks down.

SPARKLING ALONG IN the valley below is a car unaware it is driving directly into the path of the lava flow. M'hek stands transfixed watching a black cloudform advance from the horizon toward the car its molten edge snarling its fiery paws eating steadily at the world ahead. Moving about 40 mph. The herd now breathing like a bellows has formed into a circle facing outward. Io stands apart. She dips her head to her knee momentarily. Blood still buzzing with gorse she does not hesitate to believe that a masterpiece like herself can fly. Should fly. Does fly. Without a sound and by the time M'hek turns around she is aloft.

IO IS NAT King Cole soaring into the opening bars of "Chestnuts Roasting on an Open Fire" with some strange gold pepper spicking and spanning her veins and night blossoming out her head like Jim Dandy's desire from an Elvis Presley lyric. Elvis dreamed up love lyrics while he sat on the couch by his mother watching TV. "Chestnuts Roasting" was a Christmas song Nat King Cole wrote one hot summer day in Los Angeles with Mel Tormé beside the pool. Or so I have heard. Facts harbor many incongruities. Here's another. Down below in the valley G has had 4NO stop the car so he can get out and study the black and blacker air. No thought of Nat King Cole or Jim Dandy or chestnuts comes to mind when he glances up to see Io plummeting toward him at the velocity you would expect of a 400-pound object falling through space. Falling is a fact.

Soaring not a fact. But G recognizes all at once how much he loves this animal. He shoots his wings to their fullest expanse and screams once as he leaves the ground.

BETWEEN US AND animals is a namelessness. We flail around generically – *camelopardalis* is what the Romans came up with for "giraffe" (it looked to them like a camel crossed with a leopard) or get the category wrong – a musk ox isn't an ox at all but more closely cognate with the goat – and when choosing to name individual animals we pretend they are objects (Spot) or virtues (Beauty) or just other selves (Bob).

HOW OR WHAT in their minds animals call us we hesitate to think.

PROPER NAMES PROBABLY not do they even have pronouns? Do they experience the entire cold sorrow acre of human history as one undifferentiated lunatic jabberwocking back and forth from belligerence to tender care? G has thought all this before. Io's gold eyes shine at him through the blackness.

BRIGHT CURRENTS
LEAP the air. They come
together surprisingly
gently and shift direction
to a swooping curve that
heads off southward.
Winged man and musk ox
are parts of each other
although not parts of a
whole. G doesn't have
time to wonder as he
works his wings against
the thickening air why Io
is no longer falling
toward him but planing
steadily and horizontally
above his back. She
bellows. Lets loose a
great fart and poops
gloriously just missing his
head. But what is that
other sound? A sort of
succulent mechanical
knocking like a thousand
zippers undoing
themselves. He knows
that sound. He glances
up. All the bats of
Batcatraz are massed in a
moving layer between him
and Io sailing her on. A
grand day is what this is
turning into. From Io's
head and flanks the long
guard hairs stream
backward like lineaments

of an Old Testament prophet. Down in the valley below as 4NO turns the car to go back the way they came everyone looks up at a loud THUNK on the roof.

4 NO WAKES TANGLED in the steering wheel of the car. He is alone. All the car doors are open. The front of his visual domain fills at once with mountains in flame crying *More!* The flames go white. He wrenches himself back from this ravening future with a deep groan. Being prone to sudden dozes he hopes every time to wake as someone else. The word *splash* floats across. Most horrible part of ECT the little splash had the doctors not made certain promises to him he would never. Twelve treatments later awaking no different. He shrugs. Exits the car. The clinic stands deserted. Black flakes shudder down over it. He sees someone inside running from window to window. The future is already. He cannot win. He cannot help. He cannot change. He gets back in the car and closes his eyes.

FROM SILENT ROOM to silent room G searches the clinic. Cupboards stand ajar streaks mark the floor a float of dust and haste and terror just settling. And at every window the vague twilight the black flakes of this dayless day come sifting down. He listens and his hearing drowns in it. Is he outside inside or inside outside. He has no bottom to his mind and both does and does not open the note that lies tossed on his bed. *Call this number it's your mother.* Walking down a hall. Knowing this moment already. Its bark split open. Years go by. Refolding the note. Walking down another hall. A glimpse of something silver. Fear crams him. The silver tuxedo which has more than once been accepted without question is it he at the turn of the hall? Who? Without question. Call who? But that is not her number. Place where he caught his breath. Places.

TIME PASSES TIME
does not pass. Time all
but passes. Time usually
passes. Time passing and
gazing. Time has no gaze.
Time as perseverance.
Time as hunger. Time in
a natural way. Time when
you were six the day a
mountain. Mountain time.
Time I don't remember.
Time for a dog in an alley
caught in the beam of your
flashlight. Time not a
video. Time as paper
folded to look like a
mountain. Time smeared
under the eyes of the
miners as they rattle down
into the mine. Time if you
are bankrupt. Time if you
are Prometheus. Time if
you are all the little tubes
on the roots of a gorse
plant sucking greenish
black moistures up into
new scribbled continents.
Time it takes for the postal
clerk to apply her lipstick
at the back of the post
office before the
supervisor returns. Time
it takes for a cow to tip
over. Time in jail. Time
as overcoats in a closet.
Time for a herd of turkeys

skidding and surprised on
ice. All the time that has
soaked into the walls here.
Time between the little
clicks. Time compared to
the wild fantastic silence
of the stars. Time for the
man at the bus stop
standing on one leg to tie
his shoe. Time taking
Night by the hand and
trotting off down the road.
Time passes oh boy. Time
got the jump on me yes it
did.

HE BRINGS LILACS
from the bush by the
corner of her house to
which she will probably
not return this time. Or
ever and he leans his face
into them. The smell
plunges up. A vertical
smell. Wet purple
unvanquished. Her door
is shut. The ceiling tracks
flicker. *No radios no
barbecues don't honk* a
sign he saw on the way to
the hospital his mind
running like a dog off its
chain. Certain things not
decided have been
decided. He arrived on
the day after her surgery.
Has seen this corridor at
all hours. Notices again a
hesitancy in the light as if
it were trying not to shock
you with how scant it is.
He can hear the oxygen
machine through the door.
It shunts on. Runs awhile.
Shunts off. He enters.

WHEN HE IS there they
lift the stones together.
The stones are her lungs.

A WORD LIKE *rauschenberg* that allows him to not lift his pen from the paper. To bear down fundamentally. Writing itself is what he loves now the mental action the physical action. He thinks about writing all the time while doing other things or talking to people he is forming sentences in his head it keeps the white away. He can block the one stream with the other and steer around in it like a swan in reeds around the headache too which continues to rain planets within his forehead. He is rewriting his play as a novel given the futility of theater. The telephone rings. He waits for it to stop then places it inside the drawer of the bedside table with the motel Bible. It just fits. He smiles at this. As a boy he had very much liked being a crossing guard but even more liked the way the belt folded up. Placing that neat oblong into his locker twice a day is his intensest memory of school. He closes the drawer. I'd be no fucking use or comfort he said to G when the others set off for the hospital. Death to be close to makes him laugh. He can't help it. He can't explain it. It hurts everyone. *My famous philanthropy* he says with a glassy glance at himself in the mirror of the dark TV.

NOT DEATH NOT

smells. Not blood and shit on the floor. *No one should see me like this* is her main worry. So he makes her up and props her up and airs out the room before the others arrive. Here they are Sad and Ida awkwardly about the bed and G near the window. How was the trip she says to no one in particular. Her bed is as big as a speedboat and she a handful of twigs under the sheet. Her eyes are open but the gaze is downward. They all answer at once. Lava. Waterfalls. Beaches. Chattermarks. The wind. The white. The ice. What color are those shoes black or gray? she says musingly. They all pause. Gray Ida says. Got 'em at the outlet mall. Later they show her photos. G is especially proud of a shot of himself on wing amidst a hovering cloud of ice bats. The red and black composition almost operatic. She peers at it. Why did you wear *those* glasses? she says. Still later her supper tray is brought in. She pushes some Jell-O to the left pushes it back. Seems full of helpless fury. Is suddenly exhausted. We should go they say shifting about for their coats. But she looks up. Left your pearls at home today.

HER VOICE THIN
enough to see through.
She has caught him by
surprise he doesn't answer.
Of course he remembers
the pearls. They went
with the lizardskin pants.
It was the year of his
audacity the year he
decided to be *a lion of
himself* not just a bad
influence. Year he
discovered beauty (his
own) and its power.
Lizard pants girlfriends
boyfriends he had acid and
Thunderbird wine and a
battered Karmann Ghia.
His father watched him
come and go without
comment. His mother
kept a nervous smile.
They had one marvelous
afternoon together he and
his mother the summer
before he left home he
cannot now recall why
they decided to drive
along the lakeshore
looking at posh houses
and commenting on their
design. She had sharp
views on design. They
both liked a certain shade
of dark yellow that was
popular on trim. They

both liked glassed-in porches. Disagreed on trees close about the house. All the car windows open and their hair rushing around. He felt like a whole person with her that day. Perhaps it was the car – to sit peacefully side by side and talk or not talk and let time go in and out the windows. At home they all seemed caught in a badly blocked play and faces put on wrong. But now the little mother in the bed is gazing hard at him. How are you really? she says. Bad he says. Do you have help? she says. Some he says. *Get better help* she says with the last of her voice and he almost salutes. Yes ma'am he says and for a minute he believes he will do it. She closes her eyes. G is watching this exchange from near the door. You know the way out? he says to Sad. They exit.

NOT   A   CASUAL
solitude. He and she.
Oxygen machine is
wheeled in and hooked up.
Her eyelids flutter but do
not open. He sits. The
room is hot. There is a
smell. Does Proust have a
verb for this. This
struggle she faces now her
onetime terrible date with
Night. First date last date
soulmate. Old song lyrics
scamper in him. He moves
the chair back to the
window. *She's* counting
my soulmate gasps of
*make my heart beat at a
fast rate*. Oxygen. He
dozes. Waking to her avid
gaze. Wide open. She
holds in one hand the
makeup mirror in the
other a pair of tweezers.
Here she whispers. Lifts
tweezers. *Maybe you can
do it*. Taps the end of her
chin. He hesitates shrugs
pulls up his chair takes the
makeup mirror and peers
close. A beard of very
tiny white translucent
hairs all over her chin. He
moves the oxygen tube
aside and gingerly plucks
a few. Plucks a few more.

There are hundreds thousands. He hates waiting for her to wince she doesn't wince. It's alright Ma you can hardly see them he says. Her eyes fall. *Okay never mind.* Sadly she takes the tweezers back. *I look awful don't I.* No you look like my Ma. Now she winces. In later years this is the one memory he wishes would go away and not come back. And the reason he cannot bear her dying is not the loss of her (which is the future) but that dying puts the two of them (now) into this nakedness together that is *unforgivable.* They do not forgive it. He turns away. This roaring air in his arms. She is released.

OXEN STAND QUIET
under trees. Io's eyes are
closed. M'hek is in
uniform. Ida had her
sportscoat cleaned. It is a
hard blowing red evening.
The priest speaks about
the woman's good life her
exemplary son her soul's
situation in the palaces of
God. A short-notice choir
attempts "Ave Maria." The
coffin is wheeled out the
back door of the church
and onto a waiting van
someone closes the doors
of the van G watches it
drive off. And the
freedom stuns him. Here
it is the promised clearing
where great stags are
running at liberty. Say a
man has been carrying a
mother on the front of his
life all these years now
she is ripped off now his
life is light as air – should
he believe it?

NEW ADULT NIGHT

floats with face averted at the edge of town – should he beckon to it? Is this all a trick? Will Death simply stroll away amused that an intimate event (breath) should be mistaken for a law governing all beasts? Silly! Silly law! Look at the hours stacked ahead of you bales of time shining in the sun – just reach your arms in she must be there *somewhere* maybe at the kitchen table in the red velour bathrobe crouched over her coupons reaching for her smokes he half turns back – but there is only the screen door of the vestry and a row of trash cans and a bicycle. Some big old black crow just now shuffling itself off into flight.

SO WHAT TIME'S your
bus / midnight / I'll walk
you to the station / we
could get a slice on the
way / is Ray's open / isn't
Ray's always open / here's
something I wanted to ask
somebody a long time it
always happens to me /
what's that / I walk under a
streetlamp

and it goes dark they just
kind of fizz and go dark / I
get that too / does it mean
anything / I don't know /
where's G / back

at the house / doing
what / sorting stuff / we
could go over / think
he'd rather be alone /
other question / shoot /
d'you like anchovies / no /
want to share a whole pie
then I'm starving / okay /
you know once my Dad
set up a stop-motion
camera on the corner

of our house so we could
see the wind when we're
not there and cats come
and go / sounds like a
brain-on-fire kind of guy

your Dad / oh he was /
reminds

me of something / what /
she would

sing while I was weeping
if I listened she

would cease it's from a
poem / cool beans / did
you say cool beans / yes /
Ida you crack me up / do
I / so is this the 2 for 1 day
at Ray's / I sure hope
so

SHUFFLING RECIPES
COUPONS horoscopes in
a kitchen drawer he turns
up an old B&W
photograph of her posed in
dashing swim costume on
some long ago back porch.
One leg forward like a
Greek *kouros* a cigarette
in the other hand she
glows as a drop of water
glows in sun. She looks
sexually astute in a way
that terrifies him he puts
this aside and all at once
the grainy photograph the
early marvel of her life
flung up at him a thing
hardly believable! knocks
him to his knees. He grips
his arms and weeps. Pain
catches the whole insides
of him and wrings it.
Oddly now remembering
his grandmother's wringer
washer silvergreen and
upright on a platform of
wet boards in her back
kitchen beside the
washing tubs. How
carefully he'd been taught
to feed a piece of dripping
cloth between the two big
lips of the rollers while
she cranked the handle
and the cloth grabbed

forward to emerge on the other side as a weird compressed pane of itself. He hadn't known his grandmother long or well. She smelled of Noxzema. Didn't like doctors. Believed in herbs and the Bible. When the apostles walked down the street she said their shadows would heal people. His mother once told him a story about her dying. They never liked each other hadn't visited for years but someone arranged a phone call. So there they were mother and daughter on the telephone separate cities separate nights both suffering from asthma and so moved they couldn't speak. I heard her breathing I knew what it was his mother said. He looks up. He'd almost forgot about the rain. Unloading on the roof and squandering down the gutters. Rain continuous since the funeral a wrecking rattling bewildering Lethe-knuckling mob of rain. A rain with no instructions.

LISTENING TO RAIN
he thinks how strange all
its surfaces sound like
they're sliding *up*. How
strange his mother is lying
out there in her little
soaked Chanel suit. The
weeping has been arriving
about every seven
minutes. In the days to
come it will grow less.

WIFE OF BRAIN

Mothers in summer
Mothers in winter
Mothers in autumn
Mothers in spring

Mothers at altitude
Mothers in solitude
Mothers as platitude
Mothers in spring

Mothers banking their shots
Mothers grackling their throats
Mothers dumped from their boats
In spring

Mothers as ice
Or when they are nice
No one more nice
In spring

Mothers ashamed and Ablaze and clear
At the end
As they are
As they almost all are, and then
Mothers don't come around Again
In spring

RAIN HITS EVERY
side of everything. Her
deep blue raiment streams.
Her history hums along
the veins and balanced on
the beam of her. Familiar
by now with the
neckbones of night as they
shift into yet another old
dawn. Familiar to be
suspended in the lives of
others and still not. She
with her unspilled cup of
love her perfect stench her
vague knowledge of them.
Them with their plink and
twang and uncontrollable
shivering their clever
hands their tendency to
torture cats. To threaten to
be threatened is addictive
for them. She has seen a
cat with the pawpads
ripped off. And yet they
wipe one another's tears or
sweat they have good days
they roll in the snow.
Caution is best. Luck
essential. Hope a
question. Down the street
she notices a man in his
yard in his undershirt
standing looking up at the
rain. Well not every day
can be a masterpiece.

This one sails out and out
and out.

Notes

Frontispiece: *Bat* by Ida

"What big cucumbers they sell nowadays..." from Daniil Kharms, "What They Sell in Stores Nowadays" in *Today I Wrote Nothing: The Selected Writings of Daniil Kharms,* trans. Matvei Yankelevich (New York: Ardis Books, 2009) p. 73.

"A peculiar thing happened to me: I suddenly forgot what comes first—7 or 8?..." from Daniil Kharms, "Sonnet," ibid., p. 48.

"If the sky were crooked, that wouldn't make it any lower..." from Daniil Kharms, *The Blue Notebook,* in *Oberiu: An Anthology of Russian Absurdism,* trans. Matvei Yankelevich (Evanston, IL: Northwestern University Press, 2006) p. 126.

> *My heart is like a singing bird*
> *Whose nest is in a water'd shoot;*
> from Christina Rossetti's poem "A Birthday"

Reference to Proust on the momentarily impaired surface of the eye of a person who has just had a thought she will not tell you, etc., from *Sodome et Gomorrhe* vol. I, (Paris: Flammarion, 1987) p. 189.

> *She would sing while I was weeping;*
> *If I listened, she would cease*
> from Emily Brontë's poem "Hope"

NOTES

A NOTE ABOUT THE AUTHOR

Anne Carson was born in Canada and teaches ancient Greek
for a living.

A NOTE ON THE TYPE

This book was set in Minion, a typeface produced by the Adobe Corporation specifically for the Macintosh personal computer, and released in 1990. Designed by Robert Slimbach, Minion combines the classic characteristics of old style faces with the full complement of weights required for modern typesetting.